Sills

MICHAEL O'BRIEN was born in Granville, NY in 1939; studied at Fordham, the University of Paris, and Columbia; worked as a librarian; was one of the Eventorium poets, where his first book was published in 1967; taught at Brooklyn and Hunter; worked for many years editing technical publications; wrote *The Summer Poems, Conversations at the West End, Blue Springs, Veil, Hard Rain, The Ruin, The Floor and the Breath, 17 Songs, At Schoodic, Sills, Six Poems, Swift Moons Repair Celestial Losses,* and *Sleeping and Waking.* He lives in New York.

Sills

SELECTED POEMS 1960–1999

MICHAEL O'BRIEN

CAMBRIDGE

PUBLISHED BY SALT PUBLISHING
14a High Street, Fulbourn, Cambridge CB21 5DH United Kingdom

First edition published by Zoland Books 2000
This edition Salt Publishing 2009

Printed and bound in the United States by LightningSource Inc

Typeset in Swift 9.5 / 13

ISBN 978 1 84471 562 6 paperback

Salt Publishing Ltd gratefully acknowledges
the financial assistance of Arts Council England

1 3 5 7 9 8 6 4 2

to Stuart Miller

Contents

Acknowledgements

Some of these poems first appeared in *A Hundred Posters, Adrift, Agni, Aieee!, Airplane, Amazing Grace, The Atlantic Review, Bomb, Brief, Broadway Boogie, Columbia Review, The Eventorium Muse, Extensions, First Issue, Frogpond, GEM, Giants Play Well In The Drizzle, Goddard Journal, Grand Street, Kentucky Poetry Review, Là-Bas, Mail, Meal, The Mysterious Barricades, The New East Coker Toodle-oo Review, New York Times, The Nite of the Hunter, Parnassus, Prologue, Roy Rogers, SUN, Sundial, University Review, Unmuzzled Ox, West End, Works, Workshop, The World, The Yew Review,* and in *The Summer Poems* (New York: Eventorium Press, 1967), *Blue Springs* (New York: SUN, 1976), *Veil, Hard Rain* (New York: Cairn Editions, 1986), and *The Floor and the Breath* (New York: Cairn Editions, 1994).

Sills

The Falls

Nerves, those fine pianos,
plaintive as the applause of palms;
under the rain the green goes dark,
muted, difficult as desire.
The nights are white pages, the feelings accidental.
In the dream the river runs over stone
to the falls where a girl lies on her side
under the moving water. I see her clearly
through the moving water which descends the stair
to the pool below, whose floor you touch
before you let the water
bear you back to the air.

The Room

The cover put aside in the morning's heat
the bed is white, newly made, the sheet turned back
so that it holds the way it left my hand as
if a drapery had fallen from the frame.
The room is so beautiful, it is as if
I were not here, the flowering, after the
rain, the unseen grace of that which dumbly holds.
The only sound outside the open window
is an air conditioner. The fountain was
turned on once in the spring, never since. Only
one lamp is on, and in its light the objects
which support my life have a repose which we
may never know. The light falls half the length of
the wall, now cool, and above the bed there is
a Flemish nativity in a gold frame.

Summer

Another time this rain would scour
the punished head, and the body thicken
in the inclement element:
today we turn our faces to it.

Dull slate walks, silted with the dust
cars lifted from the road,
lie wet, deep blue under the rain.

The corn grows up to the river's edge.
We lie beside it,
forgetting which is the water, which the shore.

During Sickness

Vigils: a glass of water
beaded at the rim.
A day, unemphatic,
imposed on the carpet through drawn blinds.
The room is its negative image:
a furnished mirror, a vacant eye.

Persephone

a face bruised by sleep
a season where you reign among shadows

Sunday

The wind pressed against the glass.
The light upon the page was morning.

I went outside. The tide
carried the river back where it came from.

Across the island, another shore.
The shards are broken. They will not join.

Meeting of rivers troubles the water.
It does not know which way to turn.

Here the river has two currents,
one the tide's share, one that waits.

Evening resolves them. They flow south.
The moon touches the river's mouth.

Window

paper wilts in the moist air,
intentions blur, it is hard to touch—
whole days without speech.

rain flattens the exhausted flowers.
summer's machinery labors, incessant.
our bodies are close, without appetite.

the glasses sweat, the drinks are stale,
the weathervane does not move;
at windows, what savor?

from memory, conjecture,
love poems, reading Ovid
all night, the sweet flesh, the harbor

dictionaries, many cigarettes.
the nights are cellars.
we lay without sleeping.

lamps, patience.
We could not tell our pleasures apart
sleep at dawn.

Waking

Birds are breaking rocks in the airshaft.
They cry in harness, lifting the day.

Across the street
the buildings take up their space.

Surface is meeting: but here?
this poetry of minerals?

A fan labors.
A bearing destroys itself.

The cosmologies have gone to sleep.
Form is the place where we lay,

all that arrogance of flesh:
the hand finds no entrance.

An empty abundance
falls like stone.

the child's secret, who you sit down next to,
candle-flame, meal, confidence,
dawn from the other side, mailbox, river,
confusion, to be a man, to be a woman,
to deform the image, lies, health, fragility,
frigidity, to be embarrassed, brandy,
drafts, the files in their rows, news,
phone, shower, birth, the chiseled air,
money, camera, grief, signature,
Sharon, constellation, attention,
jukebox, waiting, "to cure ourselves of our images

from mayday to solstice, parades
weddings equivocal as a leaf in paradise
harpsichords falling out of windows
a chorus, a curtain of brick in the grass
generals sailing the anvil of graduation
thesaurus of platitude & disaster
potatoes mumbling down the stairs to the cellar
where the elegies are hung out to dry like photographs
Joe on the train
& the fountains are exhausted
& the light is folded & put away
& a woman brushes her hair aside with her hand as she turns on the pillow

Skin

Moving on the unstable surface
Wind ripples the cloth, the lake
A green world goes under
We turn on the day, plunge at night
Our flesh silvered over
The moon's pastoral, mirror
Gives back ourselves, only ourselves
Summer's multiplied entities
Converge in a narrow place

The swimmer exceeds his element
The children exceed their ground
The limits of the page are the limits of the world

Under the sun the pigeons arc
Print their shadows on the green
A darker green
Texture of summer in the long grass, effaced
The wind's passage, the carved stone
Effaced
The flawed glass, the river: iron
The pricks turn to ash
The room
The center of the page

Craving an image
I go to the window
A washed morning
Chimney, three gulls

Turning . . .

       Hands touching her throat
Breasts cradled in her arms

The tongue goes back again and again
To the place where the cup is bruised
Until one day you break the cup

                                  All afternoon
The grain of the table washed by the sun
Prior would sit, coffee before him
Smoke lifting from his hand, held in amber
Urging the virtues of potentiality:

                                              "Why multiply entities?"

The older part of the cemetery is overgrown
The stones fade, bleached by the sun
I trace the names with my fingers

Against this parsimony I urge your body
That page, its candor

Crossing

the ship cradles me
morning swings round
horizon so close
at the center
the nubbin
beaded with fog
that I hold on to like a child

~

the gull's descent
ends at the dome
he does not move

~

the fog silvers the green
the day is the moon's
the willow's

Another Sunday

a durable blanket
covers the city

the dogs speak French
we know the same number of words

Moira's toys
are a doll & a school-satchel

in the café
a disease of mirrors

he plays pinball
& talks to his girl

is it winter coming, or spring
the elegant cop salutes me

I read Eluard
I think of you

the bus goes to the Pantheon
the deaf speak French with their hands

Postcard

Somewhere in the Hudson Valley
a gull is looking at a cow.
A sullen wetness smoulders.
The silo would like to lie down.

Out of its kitchen, ethical as dough
& simmering like The Original Amateur Hour
spring's one-man-band
lurches across the sodden, lion-colored turf.

Jean Arp

folded in sleep a fruit ripens
stone like a vessel of milk
a shell for Venus

here women are vases
the prow of a gesture
whose shadow turns like a leaf

Deathmask: Heine

Call it repose, if a stone has repose
if the absence of suffering is repose
& the absence of everything else
except the fact of the meat of the face
brutal as a fingerprint
                              & what remains
is the shell of an intelligence
which once through these sealed lips
balanced an exact despair & gaiety
in a voice no longer homesick for Eden
because it was here, just out of reach.

Swan

Avon-on-Hudson, Babylon
camera/holding action/negative Shakespeare
"Maybe I'll take up the saxophone"
"Maybe I'll take up my bed & walk"

I come out, see my shadow, go back to sleep
What does summer know?
Odalisques without hands or feet
"Lady, walk through that revolving door again"

"They may have been happy
By the time I got there it was photographs"
Casuist of pain, it is not good for you
This bitter rosary
& you smoke too much

In Ireland, in London, in Paris, in Brooklyn
Thrift shops & women, dreams, twelve hours sleep
At a time, all the time, Ruth away
"You get bored when you can't pay attention"
My hat is out working. Health. Regards.

For Ruth

In pyjamas, you're part of the Cultural Revolution
In Texas, you listen & press flowers
In borrowed cars, you continue your travels
In the dream, you mourn, set apart
In the kitchen, you wash lettuce, praising each leaf
In winter, your nose is cold, like the babushka ladies
Falling asleep, you shake yourself down
In Salem, you take a nap on Kenny's couch, the hard sunlight falling on
    your face through the curtained window
In the chair, reading a mystery book, you invent money & a winter in
    Venice
In the window, you water your friends the plants
In the airport, you wear your new hat & blushes
In the mirror, you are a student
Working, you take long lunches with a catalogue of friends, boozy
    midtown, the artifacts of success
In cabs, you kiss me, invariably
In Japanese restaurants, you are a little girl & your mother gives you a
    bowl of *miso* before you go off to school
In your purse, a salad of banknotes
In your clear eyes
In your gullibility, "an early work of Mozart"
In your anxiety, daytime TV
In jeans, you wear your hair down & no blouse
In phone conversations, falling asleep
In the mailbox, your hideous postcards
In the living-room, you & I, waltzing to Mahler
In the morning, you drink tea & assemble the day
In New York you walk to Peter's, determinedly (I watched from the bus)
In London, you spill the broccoli & salvage it, brushing the green out of
    your hair all evening
In Paris, you send me pictures of unicorns
In the market, you finger avocados

In the night, you lean on my chest as we watch the stars come in for
    the Late Show
In the photo, your defenseless gaiety
In the window, four dogwood trees, aching to bloom

Eurydice, forget me not
in Hades' bower & bosom
where the keening idiom of reconciliation
sestina, grassy blueprint of loss
lulls a tumescent god's seed
(whose flower is death) to sleep, that a surface
bloom like spring or film—
genital heart, stammering author
of the only recurring architecture
marry gossip & legend
as we name each other again & enter
the river we never can step twice in

nullity is cinelinear, the calliopes of surrealism
arcades. arcana. the movie ends in a NJ roadhouse.
the movie ends in the 18th century.
wallclocks, misogyny, we choke on our lives
the plaster smell of a gutted building
stale & aerial. these nervous errands. these white deaths.
"Their sense of life is deficient. They have no images
to heal its contradictions." fetish & shambles, textbook, first of the day
"all the same's the luck we prove"
voices, an instant of doorways
fragmented words of the perfect poem, like a second of singing,
windblown. we grub among shadows, strangers.

Half Moon

the crazy sun
all our lives singular
(rhymes like shadows)

the day's heave
the steep bells
on the way to everywhere else

"human language is humiliation & madness"
on 9th St. a secret rain
the mumbled buildings

wit like hockey
these obstacles
a tourniquet of smoke

charm
the ghost of a form
"senseless as nature"

a postcard
a check
down the river

every candle a commodity
& drunken valentine
o shepherd

the homage is the massacre
the printing-press, the floating loan
& compost, memoir

turns, a leaf at a time
A Journey to the North Country
four-legged haiku, cranes, a day

& a day, fabulous twin cities
the chances
ambition's crapgame will never abolish

reader, any book, any October

The Note

Mythology is psychology.
The babe is the penis.
It wasn't the cigars it was the silence.
Mahler, what colors are life & death now?

"The poem is set in autumn or late summer:
the evenings were cold, there were heavy rains,
they made a fire from branches still green,
with the leaves still on them."

Early March

the world has its orders
the stoic day

that consciousness is real
though the dialect, the iron symmetries

make no spousal verse

Rimbaud

the rails of breath
now & at the hour of

massive. frightened.
busy in their lives.

gentle spirit, be appeased

Brooklyn

sky. tobaccostain. worn stone.
an egg. a bowl. sulfur.
steeple shades into air.

dull. sluggish.
smoke into thick air.
a penetration. birds wheel.

the sick air. porous. a membrane.
go under ground. not see.
the eye. the window. ceaseless.

reason & evening: a phonebooth.
summer. commerce. the long knives.
the pornographic fix.

syllogism, *ergo* riddle.
We are all junkies.
Hell is paved with images.

"Was it attempted robbery?"
"It was attempted murder."
There is no rhyme.

crux: (jukebox)
"You make me feel brand new."
"You make me feel bad news."

they put on a show in Washington.

a cage of need, a dream

                                      the ball is real

five flights up, you hear the traffic, nothing moves

a tumult, a hesitation

                                       the traffic

breathe

flat sun

                                       seaborne window

                                       tooth

& no more ecstasy

& no more reverie

                                       a windmill

                                       fishbone clouds

                                       a map of Brooklyn

between babytalk & "the Odyssey of *Geist*"
overtures syllables the Baltimore Catechism
some perpetual jukebox of the feelings sweating rhythm & blues
& the Daily News
masonry of bread & Arcadia

the pinball machine sounds like a toy piano
three garbagemen read a girlie mag delightedly in the cab of their truck
the drummer across the street unfolds the same four bars over & over
so many watchers   so many replicas
"They walk as if they were trying to hold up the rain"

death is redundant
everywhere
a smudged letter
sodden newsprint gone back to pulp in the street
nothing distinct or articulate
this compost

& the balkanization of the emotions & its proceeds
"We live in glass hats"
the bag comes with it   you could go sit in the park
the means of production is autistic
a hermaphroditic printing-press archaic as a dirigible or dodo

musicians are unpacking their gear
everywhere
testing the reeds
tuning up

"I made it out of a mouthful of air"

there is never a total scandal   life turns into life
the salad chef started out as a boxer
you don't have to dust the sky
save me the farce   in medias today
we float the vowels & the icons the spit & image
paper-route C-note parasol labyrinth century

A dream of reason calm as a garden

The air topples heavy with pollen

He thought the rails of purpose
Ended in a seedy ditch
A determination to come to nothing

The pigeon hunkers
Bright button eye moving like clockwork

The plucky ego hums like plumbing

Ophelia's ghost, like an unimproved road,
without maxim or allegory;
her snowman eyes; her pallor;
sister to Degas' drinkers, a lost sublime.

Video's fourth wall is in Hell.
She is worn as a doorpost.
She stands as if her death were a failure
in her pathetic hat

vacant and lackluster
from the water's slur and mumble;
a set of false teeth, a cracked
plate, a haggard

Indian-pipe, spring's negative,
all reach and no grasp.
Water would pour through her cupped hand.
Death's best pupil. Ask at the stone.

After a Cadence of Hart Crane

An old rummy   like Timothy Leary
zoot suit   glasshouse gang
I'll have a snort—Lent is over
those sackcloth weeks
a rosary of obsessions and errands

synapse misses   the leak of things
whiskey's clockwork and firings
the vanishing water the horse is led to

a museum   a fistfull of bills
and a seat among the stately depressives
TV busy as an eraser
old furniture   old master
your cauliflower life   your candied parish eye

In Fever

sweat beads the forehead
Tocsin of erotic memories
The river unfolds a
sunset like mercury

"Ghost! Ghost!" he cries
to the pigeons that rise
up from his feet
Under the covers a huge vague body

the size of a duchy
Toxin of erotic memories
Ten years her name in his address book
like a loose tooth

a signal fading like information, erections
useless as furniture
a vibraphone traveling
across shaken air

Jackstraws

First they take the world away
Then they sell it back

Your try to move your piece of it
Without disturbing the rest

A day without subtitles
A line at the bank

An attention blunted or dispersed
An architectural ornament

Seen out the window twenty times
Till it compares to nothing

The subway keeps no season
The woman sleeps

Locked to their verticals
Flags crack in the wind

Perceptual Difficulties

1

Sun's eye at cloud rift like the ideogram for speakeasy. Big A.
Scarlet Letter. Everything Must Be Sold. MOMMIE DEAREST. BODY
HEAT. "Is this in 4/4 or 3/4?" *New Criterion.* Old regime. A drug-
store window full of jockstraps and vitamins. Academy Safe
Warehouse Co. Century Iron Works. Punch. Once. Commodity &
Tragedy. The teeth were the alphabet. A trail of lost erections.
BRAS HALF OFF. *Whole Life Times.* The Future Is Going To Work.
The long poem hangs from its staple like meat. Furlined letter.
Poe white trash. "Don't confuse self-hatred and class war." Bashō.
Porkpie hat. Ma soeur's in de cold, cold ground.

2

Over the years and far away. Wealth is gross. One man, one art.
Memo mori. As for spelling, our servants will do that for us. Car-
rion me back, too-old virginity. A shot of Scottish. A born-again
loser. They caught him flatfooted. A bad quarto of an hour. Yes is
more. What a piecework is man. How come you paideuma like
you do do do? The handwriting is on the wall. I'll hum in a few
bars. The ghost of a Christmas repast. Language! Sandwich!
Your Imminence. Hang louche. Decalogue! Nobodaddy! Clean-
liness is next to property. Argot fuck yourself. To wit, jug jug jug.
It was a far cry from the heart. Too old to pass the mustard. The
bitter pat of little feet. I had not thought death had OD'd so many.
In the beginning was the verbiage. Piling Pelléas on Mélisande.
Jockstrap molasses. Bargain self-abasement. The joke stops here.
Accidia not. The barrenness of taxis. À demain, man. Quel deli-
catessen! I am affluent in German. Carnage must be destroyed.
Pompiers funèbres. Arson gratia artist. Jack Hughes. Christians
From Outer Space. Puns are hermaphrodites. Lucky Pierre.
Abstract pornography. Deep Throat Los Angeles. Home of the
Brave. Toujours Lautrec. The potlatch calling the Kwakiutl black.
Pornography is a metaphor. Verismo Santa Claus. Ounce is not

enough. Iliad. Theodicy. Une Semaine de Bonté makes the whole world Kim. The last lap of luxury. A blistering climax. The catalog of shits. Ars longa, 's been good to know ya. Vaya con adidas. Dressed like a horse.

3

A culture is a sort of engine for turning entropy into information. Draw your lines well and between them you can put muck. Pianos are mostly air. We're like ships that go bump in the night. You are dying of the supportable. If you sing at the table you'll marry a crazy woman. Being a man is a defense mechanism. The '60s were Clutter. The '70s are very empty. The imagination is a wound and conscience. Transcendental Red Indians. Panama is a financial scandal. Does it heighten truth? Or does it simply upholster the poetics of failure? Each of us must answer for himself. The final argument is the necessity of history. The horse knows the way. I hear you're working for the government. Start a new list. Glints, isolate flecks. Enough is enough is enough. You're killing them with overrap. There aren't any things any more. Has it ever occurred to you that my form of anarchism is domesticity? I kid you not, old sport. Never shoot over the heads of the people. Remarks is not literature. Arrest is literature. Banks for the memories. Works is an opera. Ulysses is an island. Thin ragtime. Unacknowledged mankind. Paper cuts are the worst. These seats are terrible. It's raining violence. Can I have my camera back?

song & image

1

I want to buy you a jukebox
I want to buy you a cat
I want to buy you a darkroom
I want to buy you a straw hat

I want to buy you a haircut
I want to buy you a drink
I want to buy you another room
Don't care what anyone think

Don't want to go to the movies
Don't want to go to the moon
Don't want to go to work in the morning
Stay in bed with you until noon

Walk in the park
Act like a jerk
O baby, I got those jukebox meridian sunset blues again!

2

There is a large piece of sky in the room.
You put on your yellow gown, make tea.
It takes me three days to walk to the bus.

3

You got a kiss like the Grand Concourse
You got a kiss like Chicago
You got a kiss like Chopin the Polish Scarlatti
O baby, don't you step on my blue dissuade shoes!

Thanks for the candied remarks. Thanks for the losssuit.
"Thanks for the mammary." "My sediments." "Exactly."
Sex is ephemeral, rabbinical, clockwork.
O baby, don't you step on my blue dissuade shoes!

4

ruepricks, Jerry ontology, the history of IUDs,
liberties, the pursued of happiness
blue Poles   "Tranks for the memories"
the columns that hold up the day are metaphor and translation
"Theodicy is the tip of the iceberg"
the seat of your hat   three sheiks to the wind   magi

Marcel Duchamp

The distinguishing characteristic of the dandy's beauty consists above all in an air of coldness which stems from an unshakable determination not to be moved. The voyeur then has no choice but to be both exalted and melancholy. The external world has no other interest than its transposition into winning or losing positions. The beauty is in the arrangement and the inherent possibilities. It has been confirmed that the real function of rational discourse is to imprint the master's orders in his subordinate's mind. The defects drive the machine. The simplest method is a nail driven into a vanishing point. My chance is different from your chance. He was very proud of his raccoon coat and wore it on every possible occasion. Chicago. It is a kind of rendezvous. Dictionaries are not natural. Irony is a way of accepting something. The cave paintings were movies. Don't let anyone know you're working.

Four Choruses
in memory of Douglas Wagner

1

Someone breaks in the bar across Ninth Street
stitch of the pigeon's eye   & telegraphy
stutters the morning line   whose book is hope
a virtue under the old dispensation
"Properties is theft"   "Mors the piety"
birds wheel like leaves of the same branch
& every morning I walk across town to this room
as if convinced there is some one thing to do
some snapshot or impersonation of virtue
drawn to the window like a plant
some allegorical life   & when I did
the laundry I thought   how small you are
me who played tennis with the Pope
a blind horse at a mill
& the middle term between "impulse" and "anaesthesia"
is "paycheck"   "alcohol"   a detached retina
here come the graces   with egg on their faces
an interface of resistance
fireworks   infinite hips
pure crystal   whereby I attribute
more integrity to the dead than to the living
"I have seen the future and it works"
this jargon   this romance   tinsel & exacting

2

Dishtowel stiffens on the refrigerator door
drained November sunlight
bars fill with butterflies   faces of ships
in the street a bum is reading a sock
stillness of the washed racked dishes
kettle's corolla of blue flame
"Depend upon it"   private vows, avowals
rockabye Venus   the prose of the days
shibboleth: identity   Bearded Salome
The blueprint was deferment   "Nature is no excuse"
The fin de siècle is starting early
like a nightmare idling
There are windows set in such a way
that as you pass your successive reflections
seem to be losing ground
The code is expectation   Hegelian sonatas
vanity and terror
An overdose is an accident
an argument   an operation
"Personality is a ruse"   a saxophone aria
an exoskeleton of reason   Death is long
You have escaped alone and told us
across the insipid water

3

You loved logic and music   those morning structures
as if the days could unfold like Koechel numbers
though the book of the day was work
bone labyrinth   a membrane of air
the same tune heard again & again
burnished as a relic   the worn steps thought goes in
in harness   There is another music
contour of a gone face   a sky so close
the day like a prize   the pivot eye's garland
where light is an element   a constancy
in all that weather   some trace
under the nails   sail beating like a vein
The days pour down   from their blue urn
each pearlhandled dawn
on Broad Street a girl's porcelain eyelid
the street's winking Jesus   his spikey crown
moonlight folded on a chair like clothes
darkness and rain
late flies drowsing on the windowpane
here   where there is everything instead of nothing

4

With a papery sound
pigeons take off across Washington Square
In the bank images proliferate like interest
cancer   a caricature of insight
& the screens flicker laws shoes damage
a vocabulary and consummation of distance
"You treat your body like a symptom"
an excrement   a dog's dream
"Money is the memory of vitality"
the drinker's injured guarded eyes
—not calculus   not the simplest addition
one & one & one & one
in the park the wind dismantles a newspaper
movers are folding their pads   a cloud like a bruise
darkens the sky
The songs are as battered as the books put out
in front of secondhand furniture stores
as if what persisted, intact
was the notion of commodity   our Platonic lives
adrift at evening
a stunned abstract light   in which we doubt
putting our hands into our own sides

The Days

Mahler ripens in the bookstores
Upstairs a jet is icing the sky
Across Spring Street a man pours ice from a sack
Into a bucket, precise as a drumroll
Down Sixth three buildings glow like ingots

The Morgan darkens, an old tooth
Doors of sound on 42nd Street
Where I sit in the reading room
At the window the sun comes and goes
Like a heart pumping light

     ~

The air is full of music   The radios
Abstract as a man in an elevator
We throw it away   We are money's nerves
Brushed across intersections   into the traffic

     ~

A halflife of rumor and aggression
Success is a window   The women
Tend the machines in their lovely dresses
Their examined lives are pure privation

A glaze of smiling   Information loss,
A slackening of intensity
Lesson and forgetfulness
A paycheck   A paper house

     ~

My love he has a red red nose
Blind pig of my heart
Booze rusts it like a leaf

I saw him on Sixth Avenue
On his way to work
A doorman for money

A carp on ice
Eye like a doorknob
I park this lament in his ear

~

In Schütz's Christmas Oratorio, when the angel appears to the
shepherds, "and the glory of the Lord shone round about them,"
the word for glory is "Klarheit"

glints
isolate flecks

~

Clifford Brown's tone's like a cat's tongue
this rainy Sunday
Pigeons hang out in the tree like old sneakers

~

The demon of analogy dwells in the eye. Memory finally connects
everything with everything, as if the world were an immense
pun: a broadside, against the grain, every synapse firing. The sur-
realism of everyday life, senseless and insistent as the fountain
in the museum court, when you are tired of seeing and the scent
of the flowers has come up to pillow you.

~

Pascal's case   They came at us like periscopes
with their toy drinks   all winter long
a feast of refusals

The room in the skull   a Portuguese man-of-war
floats there, who can leave it alone?

~

The working day's anemia
A drool of music in the street
Cord from headset to genitals
Segue past the stoic ghosts

Soft rain of light. The seamless buildings
Hold the dollar up to nature
The drunks in their orbits
The predestined trees counted like spoons

~

As if they were being kept after school. Drift besieged by purpose.
Another's purpose. He wanted to say, *You've graduated*. The streets
charging with meaning. The box of rags on Ninth Avenue a
woman hugging herself in sleep. PURITY IS SUPREME in letters
the size of your arm on the side of a truck.

~

Apprise and sing, the highwire act of the phone call,
a set of insides, the day's furniture and brickwork,
ghost of an enigma, a newspaper engine,
a noise in the mind

[50]

From a great distance   the late empty light

Penitential life, its imitation of machinery
its passion to do without;
so many emerging from Penn Station
where I stumbled on a pigeon's shadow.
This imitation. This siege of trash.

~

Grace as a name for what undeserved occurs. A smile put away
like a jackknife; quick alternation of sun and shadow on a day
of wind and cloud. Every gesture the rhyme of an earlier event.
The Hebrew letter of the peacock's crest. The mute, heavy cock.

~

Under the eaves a man listens to rain
in his ark of night
(all day immense clouds building weather)
drained of the images that batter his song

We come out through the mother

~

The slant light flattens the buildings
folds them like cardboard. Walking down Bleecker
as it darkens the eye settles on the
blue steady trembling of a welder's flame.

Postcards from Nambe

BIRDS AT NAMBE

like blade on whetstone
their dry, parched song

Perched, they reiterate, insistent
or, distracted, crash through weeds

though their intent is clear
Me, too, I perch and sing

～

fly drowses on the laundry
distant radio
a Spanish dance-band
plays polkas across thin air

～

ON THE WAY TO NAMBE FALLS

—You should have brought some shade
—Beer is liquid shade
A pickup nuzzles the mailboxes
We stutter past it down the washboard road

～

the windmill shifts against the grain of the wind
so the least air has a foothold

grass-grains lie like feathers on a wing

～

[52]

Days at Nambe

I wander the rooms
like my father laying the house to rest

days ordinary as dogs' names
They come at us sideways

a few sparrows on the power lines
like a beginner's tune

    ∾

The falls is a cleft
below flawless sky

    ∾

The night is a jar of slow-flowering moonlight
The eye is a horse that drinks and drinks

East Branch

bands of hemlock morning-light
shadow of moving water on the stones
high wind-sough   fiery newts
a bird like water in a pipe

a bird like two stones struck together
(bird of reproof)   through leaf-shimmer
a moth-spot of white light   sky washed
an intense blue by yesterday's rain, no vein of opal

near the spring a red leaf-colored frog the size of an eye

Three California Poems

1

The traveller does not know the names of things

Low straw flowers that look dried
Though a bee works them

Tarnished sea-burnt peonies

Stray coast cemeteries
Their downcast angels the color of salt

He walks among huge driftwood like dismantled bones
Like learning Greek

As if he could wear the world like a necklace
A fog-beaded spider's web

The only thing between him and the earth is his own shoulder
Obdurate

Hoarse needlepoint of birds at dusk their cries like tinfoil

All night the sea slamming its doors
He dreams of sleeping

2

Slate. A kind of engine
Overturning each succeeding plane.
Out past the fury at the join
Horizon's deadline calm
Sleeps in its element
Dissolving all semblance.

3

Redwoods sift light along the creekbed.
A day touched only with the eye.

The fog
Muffles the clear shape of things

Wears it away
Like the pasture's block of salt.

One thought the poem
Was a cotton I packed anger in

But when morning cracked like seed
Wit was the foot I stood upon.

Finistère

The bones of a church lie clean in the sun

Lines of an old intention
Relinquished to its elements

No one to pollard the trees
Salt roses   lichens   a rash of stone

A fox might live   in this watered light

The song the torso sings

in February
in the cold

in a thawed field

shallow pools standing
beside the corn stubble

nothing else near
all the way up

Sundown

in memory of George Quinan

This *you*
this form we keep using

like a lesson
like a ghost limb

until the stone of the third person is in place

~

What is remembered

is like a furnished room
made neat in the morning

still to be used

all that life to spare
all that refraining

each
in his bubble of speech

~

One evening we were walking around campus after supper, talk-
ing, not paying much attention to where we were going, enjoying
the mildness of the air and light. We came to a handball court
where a freshman we knew, later to become a priest, was prac-
ticing his tennis strokes. As we passed, his ball took a wild hop
and rolled across the pavement toward us. We stopped. He waited
for us to return it to him. We looked at it as if we had never seen
anything like it on earth. He looked at us. *That ball is real*, he said.

~

You don't get any older
your stillness a marker
nail come warm from the wood

We toil at joy   slow as clouds
immense

~

Loew's theater on Seventh Avenue
where I heard Billie Holiday

and the bar behind it
where we used to meet for a drink

all that sunlight and immobility
is a great hole in earth

~

Mushmouth life
its brokenness

for all that Latin
for all that harm

a blur in the clinch

all that sadness come home to the body
all that violence

~

[60]

Five o'clock. Chrysalis. The street like opening a vein. Smell of
flowers in an empty elevator. Hurrying to its event. Its quantum.
All the new buildings. Along the fault. Days like radio in another
room. Angels of nada. Their continuous arrival. Speechless and
voluble. Aimless points of impact. Beyond all likeness. *The test of
summer at its heart.*

~

Saint Anthony will not find your lost poems

I have your nail scissors
I have the marks you made in some books

a sentence broken off
fenced lot of untouched snow

~

Blue thistle from the roadside
lamp full of seeds

and a sheaf of lavender
to press in the hand

for the compact dark
at the edge of what we can do

~

To live high, up among the cornices, from exception to excep-
tion, hearing an earthly music. Six in the evening, August, a bar
on Barrow, door open to the street, Christmas lights, a horse race
on TV . . .

Cassis

Beneath its cusp
poised absence of the wave's black hollow

a lip
a gate

crucible of resemblance

shifting zero
where purposes cross

limit
threshold

every fold of the body
every fold of the day

≈

What the stones have in common is the wave
wearing their differences away

it withdraws
like gravel breathing

froth is left
salt on the tongue

rocks tossed in the spray

≈

Little tremors cross the water
little disturbances

a dress bellied by wind

a skin sometimes
a path of light

the sheen of it
wind-furrowed

~

Neither patient
nor impatient

ceaseless without purpose

in the storm
the tons of spray

where the water concludes

hang in the wind a moment
drop to the rock

~

It seems alive
creature not person

less time between each wave
but without climax

heedless of its own tumult

      ≋

The gull holds to the air
the limpet the rock

we to the days

they come and go
sunlight posted on a wall

The Passenger
for Hiroaki Sato

A crow
an old plastic bag
flaps in the wind

like monsignori
clouds proceed downstream

> *like monsignori*
> *clouds proceed downstream*
>
> *78 albums put out on the street*
> *Aeolian Vocalion*
> *the lovely names*

78 albums put out on the street
Aeolian Vocalion
the lovely names

the piglet's cabbage-leaf ears
at the county fair

> *the piglet's cabbage-leaf ears*
> *at the county fair*
>
> *rooftop cross*
> *its weight of*
> *nothing worse than clotheslines and laundry*

rooftop cross
its weight of
nothing worse than clotheslines and laundry

I wore out your memory
like a roadmap

I wore out your memory
like a roadmap

shadows of leaves
moving like water
now full summer

shadows of leaves
moving like water
now full summer

a bird that cries "*Did* you!"
all day long

a bird that cries "Did you!"
all day long

sun through shifting clouds
like a fan opening and closing
a moth's marbled-endpaper wings

sun through shifting clouds
like a fan opening and closing
a moth's marbled-endpaper wings

sound of wind indistinguishable from rain
the well mirrors sky

sound of wind indistinguishable from rain
the well mirrors sky

first drops on the windshield
like a cat's footprints
old muffler by the roadside

first drops on the windshield
like a cat's footprints
old muffler by the roadside

Information is physical
the painter said

        Information is physical
        the painter said

        right forearm sunbrown
        where it rested on the window
        the poplars' tremor

right forearm sunbrown
where it rested on the window
the poplars' tremor

damp pockets of jewelweed
blue chicory on the road to the dump

        damp pockets of jewelweed
        blue chicory on the road to the dump

        last gossamer soapsuds
        brushwork of leaves
        all that moil and fodder

last gossamer soapsuds
brushwork of leaves
all that moil and fodder

glancings
the butterfly's touch-and-go

glancings
the butterfly's touch-and-go

cowlick of grass
fingerprint
the dog's nostrils palpate the air

cowlick of grass
fingerprint
the dog's nostrils palpate the air

the feast of seeming
tight as the dirt in a carrot's knuckle

the feast of seeming
tight as the dirt in a carrot's knuckle

Corona Borealis
umbel of Queen Anne's Lace
the fog came up and ate the house

Corona Borealis
umbel of Queen Anne's Lace
the fog came up and ate the house

under its fatigues
the cricket's fancy wings

under its fatigues
the cricket's fancy wings

the chorus comes in
section by section
day heads for home

the chorus comes in
section by section
day heads for home

the wind sings in the trees
the wind sings in the lantern

                    the wind sings in the trees
                    the wind sings in the lantern

                    a plane flashes
                    now one wingtip
                    now the other

a plane flashes
now one wingtip
now the other

owls start
to question the night

                    owls start
                    to question the night

                    darkness
                    like an old blanket
                    in the trunk of the car

darkness
like an old blanket
in the trunk of the car

its mark where you slept
tepid as water

                  its mark where you slept
                  tepid as water

                  all the year's clockwork
                  to adjust
                  light's weight on eyelid

all the year's clockwork
to adjust
light's weight on eyelid

the sun is the driver
the day was before you

                  the sun is the driver
                  the day was before you

                  an older brother
                  who precedes you
                  in the powdery dusk

an older brother
who precedes you
in the powdery dusk

summer tips into fall
a pauseless music

                  summer tips into fall
                  a pauseless music

                  we go on sitting
                  on the porch
                  as the light goes

we go on sitting
on the porch
as the light goes

the lucid day
parsed like a sentence

> *the lucid day*
> *parsed like a sentence*
>
> *a subtle sentence*
> *that sends you back*
> *to its beginning*

a subtle sentence
that sends you back
to its beginning

the cat's paws are crossed
her eyes work the field

> *the cat's paws are crossed*
> *her eyes work the field*
>
> *seeming is rhyming*
> *but in the end*
> *things rhyme only with themselves*

seeming is rhyming
but in the end
things rhyme only with themselves

evening sun go down
make a spectacle of yourself

The Days, Again

Petals
drift like snow

catch the eye &
take it with them

across & down

~

a parking lot

the space where
a building was

open to the light

~

the day
contracts

the mind

jags & eddies in the
pure flow of information

waiting to go up with

the models
in the elevator

~

[72]

what consciousness is an impediment to

the space where
a day was

dismantled

~

virtuosity
of space

that ends
at a blackened

window

a long afternoon
grooming the numbers

while the light is
dispersed

~

by five
the day is something taken down

stored as value

lugging the long
syllables of its barges

a tug plows downstream

≈

days pass

a succession
of degraded copies

while outside
the light

has the force
of a demonstration

≈

several
only one

several
only one

over & over
but only one

≈

[74]

the patch of
light

on the tiles
at

the station's mouth
brightens

a
ripening plum-dust

≈

sentence
without destination

mirror
in the dark

unquickened

the world

obedient
to its orders

≈

dream of the same planet
but another life

puzzle of light and dark

blackness of a tarpaper
roof under rain

the river's pewter

∽

mirror-writing
of a bus's windows

pulling out

a canted sky
of planes that

lift and
succeed each other

a wall of weather
opposing

Earring

Summer is a glass of water
full to the brim

The surface trembles

A few shells on the table
fragile as 78s

The split seed-pods of the grass are like brushstrokes, the coastal hills a patched green. Odd voices suddenly carry over a distance, purposes murmured elsewhere. A red-winged blackbird quarters the air, a hawk rides the currents over the hill, gold lichens encrust a great tooth of stone thrust up in the field. Daily the fog moves in like cattle, filling the valleys with milk. A house in a cloud. A house in a dream. Where things change by effacement. Sundown's molten, flattened lens spilling across the horizon. The scroll unrolling so far.

Monk had his Baroness like Rilke

Hats with tiny brims
a tight little dance that brought him up from the piano

There was always a lot of silence on its way
stride articulation of the joints of a song

Who ever thinks the syntax will stop
the potlatch of the intelligence be dispersed

Ballads full of gristle splayed across one or another keyboard
sixties New York downtown

The world and its likeness
given at once

The world and the world

It is not a selection

Waves slap at the jetty like a dog's cough

I turn from the sunset
and find it reflected in an idler's dark glasses

a bauble
a rhyming

a ghost to keep off the crows

Night
world without ornament

Four Places

WASHINGTON SQUARE

So much sky in your compact-mirror
The arch gave birth to a piano
Two anti-nuns descend from the bus

AT MONTAUK

I fell asleep in the dunes, then woke
The sea still patiently playing its cards
and to disappear is the gambler's dream

MANICOUAGAN

a stuffed bird, an old tuxedo
chalk-line of the horizon
massed clouds move downstream
past tidal flats whose waters mirror
only immense and empty sky

42ND ST

"Port of Authority
Bus Terminal

Please take all
refuge with you"

the dandy you pass in the intersection
eyes like good luggage

his vest rebuffs gloom

day is burnished, a chest of medals
long silk scarf

The Terms
for Sally Gross

Be aware that there's freedom in your head.
Don't look down. Focus where the gesture ends.
The release should be fearless. The work is in the drawing close.
The two free gifts are the floor and the breath.

The end is not everything.
The weight is your own bones falling.
Follow the English.
Rest in the circle of your own arms.

The Loom

The snow's turned dross

The city's gloss wears thin
As a Bible's onion-skin

Or needle's eye

Her body
Is a kind of mirror writing

There
In its cockpit of air

Its ration book of days

Two sons
Two ways

Out

Cold quickens the ear
The lungs fill and fill

The will
Rests

At 25 below
Each step's like rosin on a bow

In the Elevator

creaks like a mast
her leather jacket
as her body stirs

Damage

One sleeps next to his shopping cart
His head rests on *The World Book of Knowledge*

One gnaws at a bone
from the trash of a meat-packing plant

One sits on a bench
lips moving like a pigeon's throat

IN THE BANK

people go hushed
to look at the money

its loaves and fishes
its decimal tongues

FROM THE YIDDISH

If a wolf stumbled in here
He'd lose his wits
He'd tear his own flesh apart

"AND IF YOU WANT RESULTS

these are results
this radiant aftermath

so many coats
on the hottest day

Radio

A forced synecdoche, a voice insisting that you infer its body from one sense only, at you, at your ear. You forget this, the sound seems to issue from a tap you control, speech poured out like water, abolishing the membrane between plenum and vacuum. Sometimes you hear radio over the telephone, a denatured music, twice-removed. Sometimes the tuner drifts, and you hear the friction between stations. A sound like the sugaring of marble. A landslide of cells.

Echocardiogram

The heart staggers on a little screen; a moonshot; a savage
ghost. The particles that form its image stream in silence, while
the ego scrambles to hang on to its own. This gets hot: someone
has gone into the dark and touched things. A kleptomaniac. The
muscle lunges and lunges, and the voyeur watches, it is his mis-
sion, rapt, insensible, one greedy eye, locked to that slammer,
keepsake, set of lips, pulsing fishmouth O

Lives of the Saints

He thought life was an arrow in search of him. His presence
seemed exceptionable, and he sought to efface it, placating or
forestalling unknown powers. He took what arrived in homeo-
pathic doses: from the window his inch of river; the offices of
pale days; a sky like ash: a kind of reflection; a kind of cartoon.
This lasted for years. One day, homesick for the body, he went for
a walk. And was lost.

A Translation

Remember it's a reproduction. Somewhere there is a house only and entirely made of words, all of which have been taken away. Beware the great systems, they are a triumph of abstraction over the world's interference. Illusion of total mobility, ubiquity. Great invisible books that dissolve like aspirin. But the world has no facing page; even a glass of water bends light. You have to find in your stash of words the ones to replace the ones you're removing. Without bringing the house down. Surrounded by a music you could drive nails with.

Chambers Street

Chambers Street ends in rain. Civic Fame's gold laurel catches the eye, but the day damps down. The man who lives in Warren Street settles in his duck blind. Four men stand like empties outside the Stanley Employment Agency. A television set left on in a shop tips its huge alphabet into the street. It is not speech but the parts of speech. Likeness joins what was separate, then the unwanted information pours in; a surd, a swarm. We round it, let the difference go. Sleep rode the faces on the subway close as the inside of an eyelid. Misery to have an abstraction for fetish. We see an image no longer there, empire trailing off in a mush of inflections, like the Confiteor; umbrella sheath on the pavement like a great black condom.

Amulet

That other music

little factory of the clarinet's action
or the guitarist's fingers

hurried
as the consequences pile up

a sound like clothes coming off

Angels

It was a way of talking about something
One was riding a bicycle up Eighth Avenue wings folded in his knapsack
One had stayed too long
Late cricket in Roquesteron unable to clear the wall

Memory

a shell
game, a

feint, day's
moon, a

box of
knives, a

box of
shadows

From an Anthology

huge drifting flower at the bottom of the pond, cloud, the sun inside

underpass, a pigeon caught in the updraft, a torn piece of paper

a sky like ash; five floors up a man on stilts is painting a ceiling

brick, asphalt; light at the limit, an old shirt you could make paper from

3 or 4 times in the tunnel radio comes back; between, there's hash

priest-like, in black, fine-featured, elegant, at the sweet lobe an earring

life with all the repeats, cradled in space, a chorus, indelible

the elevator runs through its dumbshow, its one emptying sentence

crossing noon's currents, unattached; the 3 kings of the shoe-repair shop

now the bored doorman is whistling *Dixie*, scuffling, beating the counter

a tug hauling 4 barges upstream, little heaps of syllables, smoke

impatient, though the elevator takes you no place you want to go

a typewriter ribbon unrolled in the street, a sky like lint, oatmeal

information hangs like smoke, copying itself, slowly filling rooms

the ferry sidles in from Hoboken, the day is foxed, rain-softened

talk, long-winded mantra, Memory World, the opacity of pain

winter sun, a bag of takeout too far from its source, soup gone random

intensive care, all night the tiny rotors of the IV device

window of porno tapes, 2 boxers on the screen, jabbing and weaving

the day like a parcel, its little screen, the electrons' yes or no

diligence, a plumb, undeflected rain, the body washing its hands

Formals & Bridals

Nothing to pick up. The piece of paper on the carpet is a patch of sunlight. The sentence is made of words. Shifting clouds, the casual, piecemeal gilt. Morning light has crumbed the streets. Heading out, a barge plows into the river going the other way. Wind scatters the filigree, the fine print.

~

There are words that have been injured and must be favored or worked around. Fine, hopeless work, or the hope arcane, or so fine it seems like a private club. Air curdles toward snow. Catching at mesh, base, lip, the wind lifts a trashcan into the street. The human body, abstract, steps from its shadow of newsprint. Use is not waste. Virtue is not impersonation. The day is not a labyrinth.

~

The tug of likeness, its insistence. $x = y$. That fish-scale iridescence. Otherwise an unswerving rain. $x = x$. Boxcars.

~

The eye has a corner where dark birds take off and land, folding and unfolding their wings, thrashing the air like a motor shutting down. Late spring, the blossoms' confetti. Words go into the shadow cast by my own hand. Conflagration of sunset on the database. Archaic fury and abundance to which is set the body's clockwork.

~

The practice of information. A begetting without images, a pure devising, copy and permutation, the formula rippling through cells porous as speech. Never the door that closes like a proof. The missing syllables hidden in the street.

~

And the mill of transcendence. Duplex. Mind eating mere instance. Numbers without shadows. Sun gilds the horizon, a contagion of cloud touches earth. In the dark the rain is washing the world away.

~

The jukebox repeats its old song, every detail in the place it has always had, trivial and immortal. The song struggles to immobilize life. To replace consciousness with something else. Descriptions of photographs. Days logged in by the TV, blue halo of its spore. The subway's emptied faces, all data come to rest as the car hurtles into the station. A torrent of images.

~

The elevators pass like sighs. A dream in which sleep itself is a programmed office, the sleeper compelled to the endless adjustment of the monitor's columns and rows. The clever body, at its tasks. Escalator churning in the dark. Bike messengers threading the needle of traffic. The jogger in his cloud of news.

~

Spillage. Caducity. The body's desire to let things fall. Its ceaseless dismantling and recombination. Love among the numbers. Many in conversation with themselves, coredump rappers, wired for syntax, a thread in the shambles.

≈

You're not copying something made in heaven. You're not copying someone's homework. Likeness over distance, memory over time. Fractions. Batting practice.

4 Songs

1

was carrying
a chair
on his head

I thought
the rockers
were antlers

2

sleep surrounds
it, a

fly in
amber, breath's

luggage, breath's
heavy load

3

Burger Rex
Venus Elevator
Conservative Express
The Broken Kilometer

4

A dragonfly aircraft circles the water.

Rain

ELEVATOR	CAUSE & EFFECT	BABEL
module, little cell	bumper to bumper	diaspora
CITY	GLAMOUR	APRÈS LE BAIN
cries of the hurt machines	the shine on the commodity	dawn's rosy bum
MONEY	OPERA	ALIENATION
"How do you want it?"	candy	textbook
PROPOSITION	FETISH	PENINSULA
the erotic circus	power	little cock
PICKUP	CHASER	PHOTO
a cap with earflaps	one big commercial	consent
INTENTIONS	WALKMAN	VELCRO
floats in the parade	insects eating the brain	static
MERMAIDS	TATTOO	GEOPHAGY
jukebox, mailbox	edition of one	news
RADIO	THUNDER	HASHMARKS
nooze	lumber thrown down	red-winged blackbird
NEEDLE	IMAGE	IMAGE
the hell of numbers	o.d.	fix
HORIZON	IMAGE	SLEEP
fracture of light	brothel without walls	mop up your plate
VIRTUOSO	DON Q	FADE
a man eating jello	"You're welcome."	ghost film

HOBOE	AIRSHAFT	ENTERPRISE
news	well of light	Ice Age Mechanical Corp.

WORSEN	LUNCH	CHIMAERA
parody	Yanqui Bean	Happy Hour

COMMODITY	MONEYBELT	DAYLIGHT
hegemony	codpiece	uphill sleep

Stones

What has been taken away that we have opinions in place of?
Practice. The negative. Chicory in an urn.

A world of substitutes.
A world of models.
A world of tasks.

~

Drifts through the stations of his wounds
a building waiting to be burned
a penny for your streets   your charging streets

~

The woman kneels, she has tied the leash to a fence
She combs the dog's hair with short, steady strokes like waves
He sits on his haunches, mouth open, working, eyes closed
He likes it so much he doesn't know he can stand it

~

dada was not the Mirage-Palace
dada was not the bagman of the infinite
dada was not the pimps of death
dada was not our Thirty Years' War

~

Looking for a job in Vallejo's blue suit
New York's iron snow is worn as a sink
and to walk through it is not to subscribe to it he thinks
as whoever's behind him in the revolving door takes over

Rubric

lost in the grain of the crowd
the office of numbers

that life
to which one has tickets

tiles brightening
from the oncoming train

Achill Island

Turf-ditches each side of the road like an ogham inscription;
sheep, their day-glo markings and minstrel faces;
small birds bunched on a powerline,
hillside crossed by cloud-shadow;

a plant with leaves the size of an elephant's ear;
deserted houses, all striving worn away;
a crow and a ewe, off-rhyming;
on close-cropped ground tiny yellow four-petaled flowers;

stone-colored sheep asleep in a field; acrid peat-smoke;
trees the wind has pushed all one way;
a butterfly the size of a thumbnail, paisley one side, deep blue the other;
words to look up, *gorse*, *tarn*, *bog*; shells from the strand.

Winter

The snow's di-
agonals
drift across
the imagined
space of the
city's co-
ordinates

& what stirs
as if to
meet them is
the desire
for oblit-
eration:
that it all

come down, not
just the snow
but the space
& the laws
that predi-
cate it, that
it be ef-

faced, along
with the con-
sciousness of
its devis-
ing: blackout,
sleep, the wear-
ing away

of every
thought of who
we are or
meant to be,
the very
zero of
our setting

forth, lost in
that hushed, crys-
tal softness,
whispered noth-
ing, drifted
smudge of a
wet eyelash.

At Schoodic

Ocean has
no eyes

for us,
stares us

down, jumble
of rocks

& water,
a billion

syllables, an
old confusion.

～

Past the
island

dense with
pines the

lobster-
boat with

its cloud
of gulls

enters
the bay.

～

Fisher of
passages,

shallows &
inlets,

patient, the
heron turns

sideways &
disappears.

≈

Each slow
wave, lifted,

climbs its
staircase of

rock, crowding
in, hurling

its lace
in sprays.

≈

Full moon over
water, the

small change
ferried across.

≈

Day glows
through fine rain

wave-glint
bright with spume

fog e-
rasing the

night, sea
changing rooms.

14 Songs

1

the dogwood's
rush

to surpass
itself

every surface

pressed into flower

2

gnomon
shadows the park

sundown
eases darkness from river

though façade
glow like theory

3

What he
thought were

two tiny
balls of

mercury rolling
along the

bar were
in fact

a passing
bus's reflections

in his
glasses' lenses.

4

sometimes the
period
is the syl-

lable : ghost
beat, the sax-
ophonist's

finger point-
ing up to
the unsound-

ed note : vow-
el, promise,
IOU

5

a banging
in the pipes

a cotton
sky, host to

numbers, the
syllables

counted like
seeds, tongue &

groove hidden
in the wall

6

brush off the subway's
mask of sleep : scuds &
gusts of rain, the

wet, pearly traffic, steady
burn of neon in a
luncheonette window

7

Clouds like
opera.
      On the
train the boy
cups the ball

in the
socket of
his lacrosse racquet.

Outside the
bar a
man tugs at
his vest, soothing
himself down.

8

sudden, rank,
the paper-
whites burst the
green sheaths of

their blossoms,
unfold through
the declen-
sions of light

9

both the music's
pure dream of it-
self, and the ma-
chinery of

its making: sound-
less keyboard where
David practiced
In Nomine

10

all the names
are given
names: sky,
cauldron, tun-
nel of love

11

The sound of
crickets pours through

the day: dry
creatures among warm

stones: one fell
asleep cupped in

my father's hand

12

sleep honey-
combed with dreams

a vowel
to ride on

13

the man mending
his sidewalk, sprinkling

it down, offhand
as a priest

14

and
the sills

of
evening

A Pillow-Book

Grasshopper can't keep her mind on tomorrow.
— RACHELLE GARNIEZ

"You have to be optimistic in *this* life," the man says to his companion, slightly emphasizing the *this*, as if there might be some other life in which one could be pessimistic or hold no opinion.

"Paper cuts are the worst."

"See how you act silly?" she says to her boyfriend. "Just *stay* here."

We wanted to use the power of a computer to collapse time and distance, which are enemies of a highly decentralized service organization. . . .

Parodies of desire. Paradise of desire.

"Purgatory is where you get it right."

Sayings of my mother: *Whom the Lord loveth He chastiseth. A soft answer turneth away wrath.*

Universal Maintenance. The whole show run out of a very unassuming storefront on West 41st St.

Deliquescent Father M., his blunt, uniformed body, all expression forced up into the head, his melting eyes and orgasm voice.

The man walking toward me struggles to stuff a folded newspaper into his overcoat, all I can see is the huge headline: GUILTY.

I tell S. I've been three weeks in the country and have only a *haiku* to show for it. She says, "That's less than a syllable a day."

"Water will reflect anything."

Sometimes the music is breathing for you.

Imagine a kind of permanent office.

The months are capitals.

House of gold. Ark of the covenant.

The immobility of the drinking life.

That handspan of nothing between ribs and pelvis.

TV. Its deck of images, its routines.

Trinity Churchyard. A man reads his newspaper among the graves.

Rocks "older than air."

The *golem* of information.

The embarrassment of the dead.

"Irony plays for a draw."

The hell of numbers. A stammering of signs.

Death has a bone to pick with us. Celibate death.

"It made sense while I slept."

Xerox days. Graffito'd on the wall, five pricks like periscopes.

The man my father knew who'd had a stroke and could say only *God, what a day!*

The escalator reciting its poem at Lexington Avenue.

On 23rd a limping collie, a defective metrical foot.

Out of the tunnel, grey spider-sun over wintry Jersey marshes.

Sunset flashing in ranks from an office building's monument windows.

"Prigs need to be blameless."

A headache painstakingly dismantled, its pieces numbered, crated, shipped to another part of sleep.

Days in the attic, arranging the parts of the body. The house that repression built.

President of his class. His lemonade stand.

Erections salute dawn. All that old chivalry, like a horse pressed in a book.

Freedom Check Cashing Co.
Empire Restorations
Majestic Interior Demolition Co.
Indelicato Plastering Co.

Mirror in the dark, unquickened, the rain washing the world away.

The Instructions

a shell, a
ring, a game
of idleness, inviolate
summer beneath its
towpath of stars

*What was done in sleep
must be done again,
once on each side* (tho
the best join's unseen)

oil-slick irrides-
cence of speech, *a noise
in the mind*, a poem
all instance, charged as
the air before rain

forsythia's first,
sparse punctuation,
yellow on black: restless,
thunder the billion-
aire gathers its load

Arthur Dove

From its cocoon,
a seed, a source,
sun's annular
rings wash to their

limit as horn
probes fog, that
soft, capillary,
germinant note.

In Memory of Frank Kuenstler

Little bones of
the ear, house built

of air, cloud-wraiths
cross hillside, wind

lays shadow on
water, leaf-shape

on wall, day bears
down, seamless, last

bird's slow song, a
pipe reversed, con-

stellation of
four tones, shifting

For Iso & Susan

Tufts of pale-
violet
asters spring
from creviced

rock : tide-race,
faceted
world : planet
wheels to dye

six leaves still
warm with sleep :
cormorant,
heavy-winged,

a vector,
crosses the
bay's calm,
mazy water.

Trains Going By

An extra-dry martini
straight up with a twist and four
quarters.
      He speaks to no one,
drinks slowly, feeding coins to
the jukebox, lead-footed swing
tunes from the '30s.
                Ain't no-
body's business if I do.

Late August

No wind. Each leaf in
eternity. A
question-broken dream-
speech approaching its

limit. Flail of the
cicadas, that dry,
vacant sound. That husk.
Fury! Shipwreck of

sunset, waterfall
of the descending
escalator, its
fixed, archaic

gaze. Pulse of light. Lip
of the visible.
Eye to sky's quarter
where the lightning is.

Applecross
for Roger Little

At mountain's foot
the wind finds you

lake of shadow

stroke of reeds on
silver water

foxgloves' tall bells

sheep still as stone
as lichen on stone

the wind finds you

A Quarry

So much eyelid in a girl's downcast gaze
Washington Square powdery with dusk

cicada-song of the nervous system
crossing the day's vacant places

37 floors of parallel lives
little bell of the coffee-cart

Landowska's harpsichord, a clatter of wings
dune grass another part of the dark

the speck of perception

that ignites
in all that weather

heron, march-lord

breath's seesaw
spray-blown rainbow

down in the remainders a
circle whose center is a baby the size of a book

slow as leaves turning

Stations

Patience of the lost, going
through their ruins: ageless white-
haired high-browed black man in the
59th St station, wild
eyes nowhere, opening &
closing a filthy Bible
like a valve. Like breath.

～

Intent, a
man is talk-
ing to a
machine to
a machine.

～

Suspended purpose of
waiting rooms, where
dread accrues, its film of dust

～

On the steps to Manhat-
tan Community
College a statue of
Icarus starting to
come apart like a
747.

Horses standing in rain.

A jet passes
like torn paper.
Moon's calculus,
tumult on bay &
inlet, the
honeycombed rock.
Sky assembles its
darknesses.
The nerves
roar.
      Thun-
der ga-
thers its
ashes.
      Autumn
pours down.